INTRODUCTION

Stratedice is a book of dice games that will help exercise the brain. Stratedice contains fifteen fun, mathematically challenging dice games that provide many opportunities for players to fine tune their decision making and logical reasoning skills. Players (sometimes referred to as "DICERS" throughout this book) must practice addition, subtraction, multiplication and division with a STRATEGY TWIST. To maximize success players must apply their knowledge of probability concepts. In other words, you need to have a plan in order to outwit your opponent. By thinking logically, you can apply your math knowledge and use careful reasoning to solve the games and ultimately beat your opponent (or yourself).

So...

Get rolling and get STRATEDICED!

Take a chance, shake up the dice and stratedize your next move!!

You never know, you might be the next stratedice expert! A world-famous

"DICE WIZARD"!!

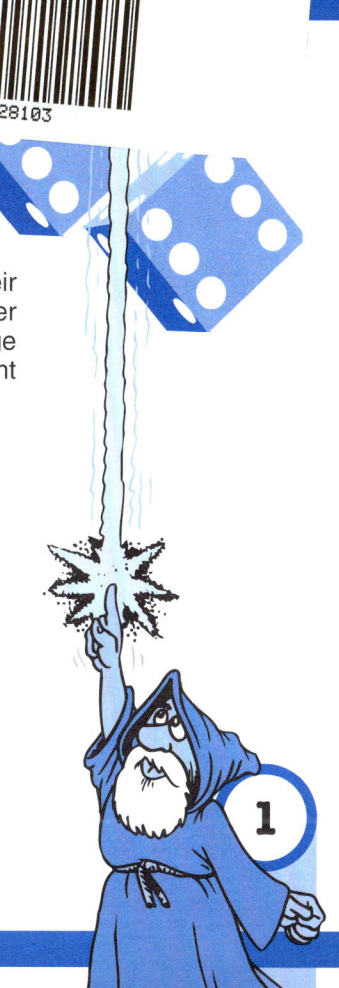

Jane and Joanne

TABLE OF CONTENTS

STRATEDICE 3
TRIPLE PLAY 5
LEAP FROG FOR TWELVE 7
ROLL'N ON PLACE VALUE..9
"36" 11
PROBABILITY PLAY OFFS 13
EVEN THE SCORE...15
TRINGO 18
DON'T HANG LOOSE! 20
KNOCK YOURSELF OUT! 22
SQUARE DOUBLING..25
CHANCE 27
HIGH ROLLERS 29
DOUBLE TROUBLE 31
4 BY 4 32
HORSE RACE 34

STRATEDICE

2 DICERS 2 PLAY

This is a game for two Dicers to play at one time.

TO BEGIN

Each player rolls eighteen dice of their own colour. The player with the most number of sixes rolled begins the play of the game. If both players roll an equal number of sixes then the player with the most number of fives begins the game.

THE GOAL

The goal of the game is for each player to build rows or columns of three or more dice of their own colour in any direction ie., horizontally, vertically, or diagonally. At the same time, players attempt to prevent their opponents from doing the same.

Each player takes a turn rolling one of their coloured die and placing that die in any position in the tray. Players continue to place their dice into the tray until all spaces are filled (see example 1).

TO SCORE

Each Dicer adds the face value of all rows or columns of three or more dice of their own colour and totals these sums. The player with the highest score wins.

Example 1

Player 1 rolls a 5 and places it on the board.

Player 2 rolls a 3 and places it on the board.

Player 1 rolls a 2 and places it on the board.

Player 2 rolls a 6 and places it on the board.

Player 1 rolls a 4 and places it on the board.

At this point, Player 1 has three in a row. This will count as 11 points (5+2+4) at the end of the game.

3

STRATEDICE (CONTINUED)

POSSIBLE STRATEGY

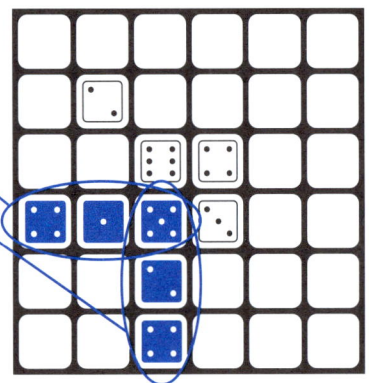

In this example, Player 1 has used the 5 die both vertically and horizontally and is now able to score twice with it.
(4+1+5=10 and 4+2+5=11)

Example 2

One strategy might be for players to count sixes and fives more than once by building an intersecting row and column with that particular die (see example 2).

Remember, you can improve your score by using high numbers to score and low numbers to stop your opponents' strategy.

VARIATION I

Play a "golf-like" variation of the game where the goal of the game is to avoid getting three of your own colour in a row. Any three or more in a row of your own colour count against you. After adding up the sums, the player with the least total wins.

VARIATION II

To challenge yourself, try multiplying the numbers when totalling your score. Grand total scores can be calculated using a calculator. The Dicer with the highest score wins.

TRIPLE TRAY

TO BEGIN

Players use one tray divided evenly so that each player uses only half of the tray. Players select their own colour of dice. Player one chooses one die, rolls it and may place it into any space on their side of the dice tray. The die is placed into the tray with the same number showing as was rolled. Player two now rolls and the players alternate until the tray is filled.

THE GOAL

The goal of the game is to build rows and/or columns of at least three dice of your own colour in any direction ie., horizontally, vertically, or diagonally. The players attempt to build sequences of **repeated numbers** ie., 3 twos or 3 threes in a row, etc. (see example 3).

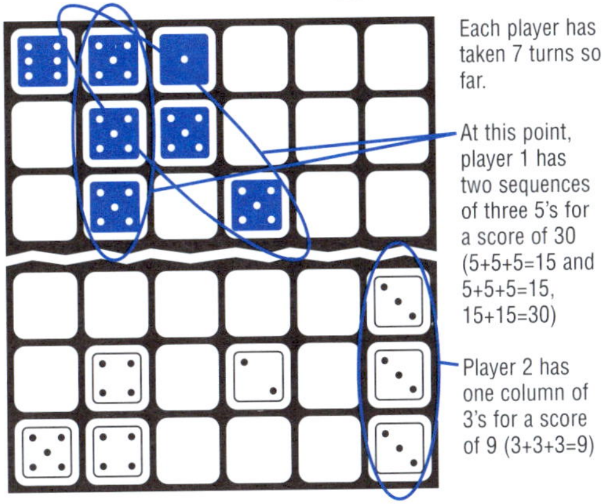

TO SCORE

Each player adds the face value of all rows of three or more dice with a repeated number pattern. The player with the highest score is the winner.

Example 3

Each player has taken 7 turns so far.

At this point, player 1 has two sequences of three 5's for a score of 30 (5+5+5=15 and 5+5+5=15, 15+15=30)

Player 2 has one column of 3's for a score of 9 (3+3+3=9)

POSSIBLE STRATEGY

One strategy for players may be to count sixes and fives more than once by building more than one sequence with them.

5

TRIPLE TRAY (CONTINUED)

TIP

This game is great for Yatzee practice! Practice repeated addition and counting multiples.

ie., 3 + 3 + 3 + 3 = 12 or 4 x 3 = 12

VARIATION: A RUN OF THREE

At this point in this variation of the game, player 2 has scored in two places. His total is 18 points. (3+4+5=12 and 1+2+3=6, 12+6=18)

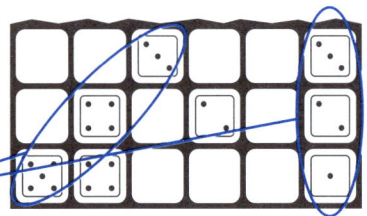

Example 4

The goal of the game is to build rows and/or columns of three or more dice of your own colour, in any direction ie., horizontally, vertically, or diagonally. The players attempt to build rows of numbers in sequence ie., one, two, three or three, four, five, etc. (see example 4).

TIP

Players may want to keep a running total of their score as they play.

POSSIBLE STRATEGY

Don't forget for a "Triple Tray - Double Play" (say that fast 3 times and you're the new president of our Dicer Club!!), you can count any die more than once by building a new sequence in a different direction (see example 3).

LEAP FROG FOR TWELVE

TO BEGIN

The dice tray is shared between both players. Each player rolls six dice of their own colour and may place them into any space of the first row closest to them. Each player then rolls their second set of six dice by rolling them one at a time and placing them from left to right in sequence in the second row of the tray closest to them (see example 5).

THE GOAL

The goal of the game is to create rows or columns of three dice that when combined by any operation, equals twelve. To move, players may jump over their own colour of die into an open space or move a single space in any direction, into any open space. Players alternate moving or jumping over dice of their own colour until one player says "Freeze Frog" outloud. Their opponent may now take their last move and the play ends. Players must make a minimum of three moves before saying "Freeze Frog".

When both players are finished rolling, the tray should look something like this.

Example 5

LEAP FROG (CONTINUED)

TO SCORE

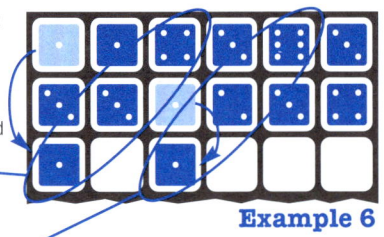

Looking only at player 1's moves:

First, player 1 jumps a die and can now make 1x3x4=12.

Then, player 1 moves a die to make 1x2x6=12.

Example 6

Players look for all rows or columns of three dice that equal the target number of twelve. Players earn one point for each correct combination (see example 6).

VARIATION I

Dicers may vary the target number ie., fifteen or twenty etc. and may allow four dice per combination.

VARIATION II

Dicers may decrease the level of difficulty and allow a minimum of two dice per combination to equal a target sum of seven.

VARIATION III

If a Dicer misses scoring one of their own combinations and their opponent notices, their opponent may earn their missed points and add it to their own score.

POSSIBLE STRATEGY

When rolling and placing your first six dice at the beginning of the game, you may want to mix up your numbers. This may allow for a variety of combinations. Experiment and be a "Spicy Dicey" risk taker!!

ROLL'N ON PLACE VALUE

2 DICERS 2 PLAY

TO BEGIN

Dicers select their own colour of dice. The dice will be rolled alternately one at a time by the players throughout the game. A total of three rounds will be played (see example 7).

THE GOAL

The goal of the game is to be the player who creates the largest six-digit number in each round.

TO WIN

A Dicer must be the first one to win two out of three rounds. To start the first round player number one rolls a die and selects the best place value position in their row. For example, if player one rolls a two, the "tens" position might be selected. Player two now might roll a five and place it in the "ten thousands" position of their row. Once a die is placed in any place value position it cannot be moved. Remember, this is a game of chance. It depends on chance whether you throw the number you want on the die. Be a risk-taker and make a calculated guess. The more you play, the better you'll play. Players alternate taking their remaining five rolls, each building their own hundred thousands number - keeping in mind the goal of the game is to create the largest number possible.

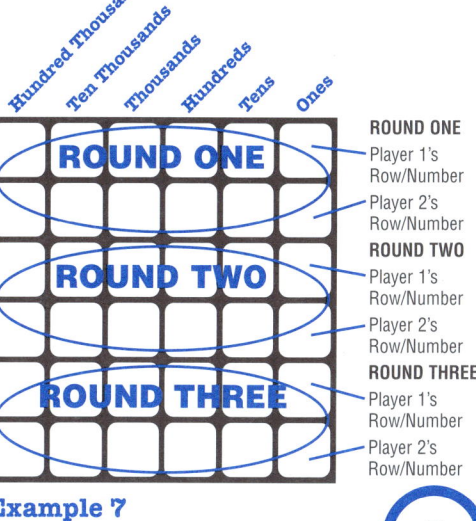

Example 7

ROLL'N ON PLACE VALUE (CONTINUED)

Player 1 rolls a 5
Player 2 rolls a 4
Player 1 rolls a 3
Player 2 rolls a 4
Player 1 rolls a 6
Player 2 rolls a 5
Player 1 rolls a 4
Player 2 rolls a 5
Player 1 rolls a 2
Player 2 rolls a 1
Player 1 rolls a 4
Player 2 rolls a 3

Player one's number is 645,342 which beats player two's number 315,445.

Example 8

Once all dice have been placed, players say their numbers out loud and compare them to determine which player has made the greatest hundred thousands number. This Dicer wins that round. In example 8, player one wins round one. Play continues into round two and if necessary a third round is played to determine the overall winner.

VARIATION I

To decrease the level of difficulty players may roll less dice ie., only four dice per player to build a thousands number or three dice each to build a hundreds number.

VARIATION II

Dicers can agree to change the goal of the game and now attempt to build the smallest six-digit number in each round. A roll of 1 or 2 is now considered a "nice dice" roll! The lowest number you could possibly roll would be 111,111. What would the probability of that be?

2 DICERS 2 PLAY

"36"

TO BEGIN

The tray is shared between both players. Dicers select their own colour of dice. Player one rolls two dice, multiplies their numbers and verbalizes their product (answer) out loud. Player two now does the same. Dicers compare their products and the player with the greatest product places their two dice into the first two spaces on their side of the tray. Their opponent places their two dice aside and they are not used again (see example 9).

THE GOAL

The goal of the game is to roll two dice that when multiplied equal a greater product than your opponent. Dicers continue rolling two dice of their own colour, multiplying and comparing products until all thirty-six dice have been rolled. If both players roll identical products, players may choose to re-roll to break the tie, or may both place their dice into their own side of the tray.

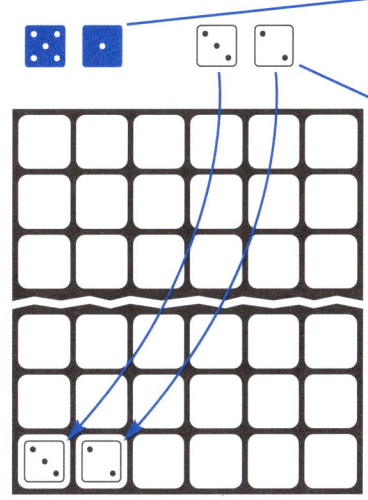

Player 1 rolls a 5 and a 1 which when multiplied equal 5 (5x1=5).

Player 2 rolls a 3 and a 2 which equal 6 (3x2=6).

6 is greater than 5 so player 2 wins this round and puts their dice on their side of the tray. Player 1's dice (5 and 1) are set aside.

Example 9

TO SCORE

Each player counts the total of their own dice placed into their side of the tray. The player with the most dice is the winner.

"36" (CONTINUED)

Hey Dicers, can you guess why we call this game 36?

Hint: What's the highest product you can roll?

VARIATION I

To decrease the level of difficulty players add their two dice together and compare sums (answers).

VARIATION II

Players subtract their two dice and compare differences (answers). Smallest difference wins.

VARIATION III

A more challenging variation would be to roll three dice at a time and combine the three numbers to come up with the greatest possible answer.

A DICE TWIST

Dicers could predict whether they think their sum/difference or product will be an even or odd number. If correct, they earn an extra point.

PROBABILITY PLAY OFFS

TO BEGIN

The dice tray is shared and divided equally between both players. Each player selects their own colour of dice and rolls all eighteen dice at once. Dicers can place their dice into any of the spaces of their three rows. Problem solving strategies and an understanding of probability will help players choose the best position for their dice (see example 10). Player one now removes and temporarily borrows two of their dice to roll a target number (sum). Once this target has been determined player one returns these two dice to their original position. Players now take turns using one die or a combination of two or more adjacent dice and any operations to equal the target number. When a player does this, they can remove the dice that when combined equal this target (see example 11).

2 DICERS 2 PLAY

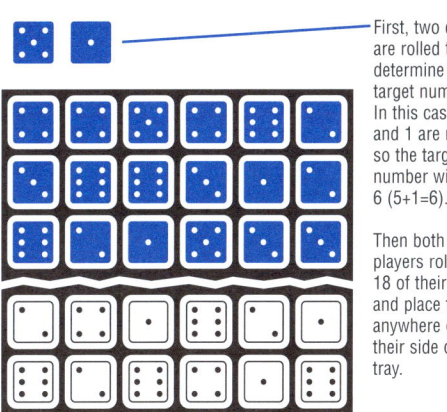

First, two dice are rolled to determine the target number. In this case, 5 and 1 are rolled, so the target number will be 6 (5+1=6).

Then both players roll all 18 of their dice and place them anywhere on their side of the tray.

Example 10

Remember, Dicers... you can add, subtract, multipy and divide all in one combination.

☆Watch this move for the bottom row of dice:
(3 + 5) - 3 - 3 x 1 + 4 = 6... Yahoo! All six dice could be removed!

13

PROBABILITY (CONTINUED)

THE GOAL

Looking only at player 1, the following equations may be made. The following dice would then be removed:

(4 - 3) x 6 = 6

(5 - 4) x 6 = 6

6 x 1 = 6

(6 - 4) x 3 = 6

3 + 2 + 1 = 6

No more combinations can be found, so player 1 is left with 4 dice.

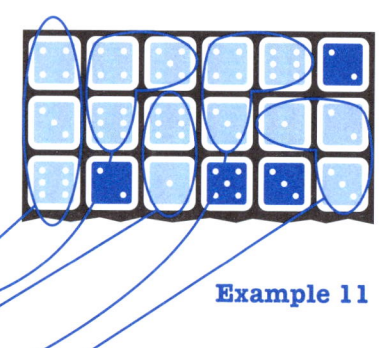

Example 11

The goal of each round is to equal the target number using as many dice of your own colour as possible. Within any combination, each number (die) can be used only once.

Play continues until all combinations have been removed. The player with the least number of dice remaining in their side of the tray is the winner. (Remember 6 is the target number for this example).

In example 11, player one has 4 dice left. Is this the least amount of dice that could have possibly been left in the tray? What other moves could have been played to improve this score?

POSSIBLE STRATEGY

One possible strategy for players would be to explore the probability of sums when rolling two dice. The placement of the dice into the tray at the start of the game should reflect this. Players would maximize their chances of targeting the numbers by placing their dice in combinations that equal or come close to equalling the most probable target rolls.

EVEN THE SCORE

TO BEGIN

Players share the tray by dividing it so each player has one half. Both Dicers select their own colour of dice. At the same time, both players fill their three rows by rolling one die at a time and placing them left to right in sequence on their side of the tray. Once the tray is filled play begins (see example 12).

2 DICERS 2 PLAY

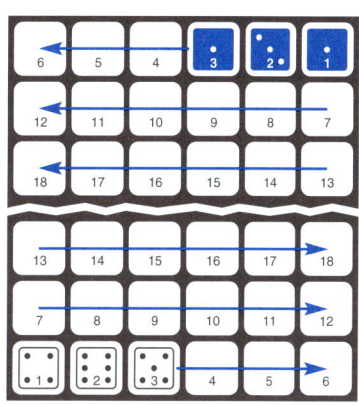

Players take turns rolling one die and placing them left to right on their side of the tray.

Example 12

15

box cars and one-eyed jacks®

EVEN THE SCORE (CONTINUED)

THE GOAL

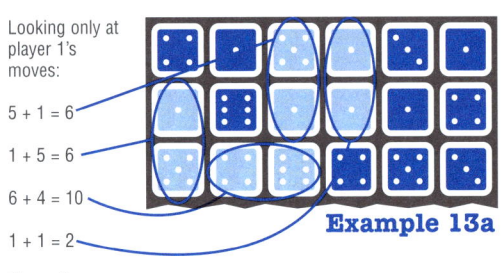

Looking only at player 1's moves:

5 + 1 = 6
1 + 5 = 6
6 + 4 = 10
1 + 1 = 2

Player then jumps a die and can now take 4 + 4 = 8.

Example 13a

Example 13b

The goal of the game is to remove two dice of your own colour, that when added equal an even sum. Players alternate turns removing adjacent dice and verbalizing their even sums. If a player is unable to find an even combination they may move one of their die one space, into any open space, or jump over one of their own coloured die to the next open space. This counts as that player's turn. Play continues until all possible moves have been taken (see example 13).

Keep in mind that players alternate turns. When removing dice it is important to look for even sums of dice that are vertical, horizontal or diagonal to each other.

THE WINNER

The winner is the player who has the least amount of dice remaining on their side of the tray at the end of the game. If Dicers tie ie., have the same number of dice remaining in the tray, the player who took the **least** number of jumps and/or extra moves into open spaces is the winner.

EVEN THE SCORE (CONTINUED)

VARIATION I

Dicers could remove two dice that when multiplied equal an even product.

VARIATION II

Players could remove three adjacent dice at a time that when added equal an even sum or when multiplied, equal an even product.

VARIATION III: ODD MAN OUT

The goal of any of these games could be altered so that players are attempting to equal an odd sum or product.

TEACHING TIP

During the play Dicers may want to tally their extra moves in case of a tie.

TRINGO

When all dice have been rolled, the tray should look something like this.

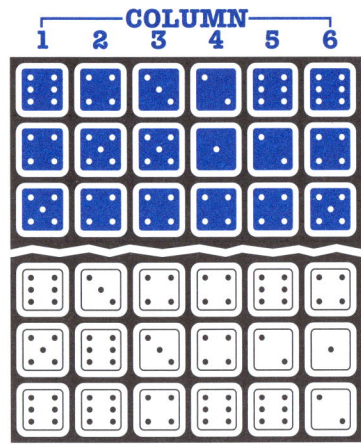

Example 14

TO BEGIN

Players share one tray and divide it equally. Dicers select their own colour of dice. At the same time both players fill their three rows by rolling one die at a time and placing them in any sequence on their side of the tray. Once the tray is filled play begins (see example 14).

2 DICERS 2 PLAY

THE GOAL

The goal of the game is to be the first Dicer to have five empty spaces in a row on your side of the tray. Two extra dice are needed: one die to determine the column from which dice will be removed; and one to determine the target number needed to be reached by using the dice in that column.

A RULE TWIST:

Dicers may choose to roll only one extra die, to set the target number. Instead of rolling a die to determine the column, Dicers both start at column 1 and continue on to column 6.

TRINGO (CONTINUED)

EXAMPLE (see example 15)

Player one rolls a 5 (the column) and a 3 (the target). Player one now searches in their column 5 for any single die or combination of dice that reaches the target number 3. Any operations may be used. Player one finds that 6 ÷ 2 = 3 and so the 6 and the 2 are removed.

Player two now rolls a 4 (the column) and a 2 (the target). Player two searches in their column 4 for any single die or combination of dice that reaches the target number 2. Player two finds that 4 + 4 - 6 = 2 and so both 4's and the 6 are removed.

TO WIN

Players continue alternating turns until one player has five empty spaces in a horizontal row and says "TRINGO" out loud.

Player 1 rolls a 5 and a 3.

Searching column 5, player 1 finds 6 ÷ 2 = 3 and can now remove the 6 and 2.

Player 2 rolls a 4 and a 2.

Searching column 4, player 2 finds 4 + 4 - 6 = 2 and can now remove both 4's and the 6.

Example 15

VARIATION I

Three extra dice are needed. One is rolled to determine the column, the other two are rolled and added together to determine the target number.

DON'T HANG LOOSE!

TO BEGIN

Players use one tray divided evenly so that each player uses only their half of the tray. Players select their own colour of dice. Players will be rolling six of their dice at one time.

THE GOAL

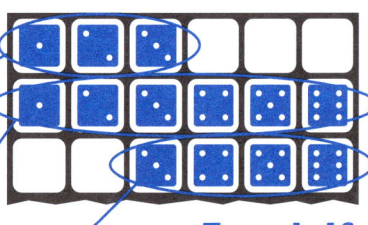

Example 16

WINNING ROWS

This row has a 1 in it and has 3 numbers in sequence to score 6 points (1+2+3=6).

This row has all dice in sequence and scores 21 points - the highest score possible (1+2+3+4+5+6=21).

This row has a 6 in it and has 4 numbers in sequence to score 18 points (3+4+5+6=18).

Dicers are building rows of number sequences from one to six. Each row is built in three rolls maximum, per turn. A number sequence must have at least three dice within their sequence and it must include a one, a six or both. Otherwise **it's hangin' loose** and these dice must be removed from the tray and placed aside (see examples 16 and 17).

To start a row, Dicers roll six dice at one time. Players alternate rolling their dice and building their rows. If a player places a die or dice into their tray and chooses to pick them up and re-roll them before their three rolls are over, they may do so. Players need to use good rolling strategy when choosing which dice to keep and which dice to re-roll in an attempt to build the longest number sequence possible.

2 DICERS 2 PLAY

DON'T HANG LOOSE! (CONTINUED)

EXAMPLE (see example 16)

The following is an example of only Dicer One's first row:

First Roll: 1, 1, 2, 4, 6, 6 — Dicer chooses to place the 1 and 2 into their tray and picks up the other 1, 4 and two 6's for their second roll.

Example 17

Second Roll: 1, 3, 3, 6 — Dicer chooses to place the 3 into their tray and picks up the 1, 3 and 6 for their third and final roll (this player's sequence now has 3 numbers in sequence so it "qualifies" for scoring - it's attached to the 1 die!).

Third Roll: 3, 5, 6 — Dicer cannot use any of these dice so the sequence of 1 to 3 is complete and their first row is built for a score of 6.

LOSING ROWS

This row has a 6 in it but doesn't have 3 dice in sequence, so it scores 0.

This row has a 1 in it but doesn't have 3 dice in sequence, so it scores 0.

This row has 4 dice in sequence but doesn't have a 1 or a 6 in it, so it's "hangin' loose" and scores 0.

TO SCORE

To score, Dicers must have at least three numbers in sequence and must have at least a one, a six or both to count. Dicers add up the face value of all "counting rows" and the player with the highest overall score wins.

KNOCK YOURSELF OUT!

Players set up the tray as shown.

Two extra rolling dice

Two extra rolling dice

Example 18

TO BEGIN

Dicers use one tray divided evenly so that each player uses only half of the tray. Each player needs 6 dice to place in the tray and 2 extra dice for rolling. Players arrange their colour of dice in the tray as shown in example 18. The dice are arranged in this position with the numbers 1 to 6 showing. All other dice are placed to the side and are not used in the game.

2 DICERS 2 PLAY

KNOCK YOURSELF OUT! (CONTINUED)

THE GOAL

The goal of the game is to be the first Dicer to remove all six of their dice from their side of the tray. To determine who goes first each player rolls the two extra rolling dice and adds them together. The highest sum goes first.

Players alternate turns and play as follows: The two extra dice are rolled on each player's turn. The dice may be either added for a sum or subtracted for a difference. The answer must be a number from one to six. A Dicer can choose which operation to perform and remove only one die per turn. If the die removed is a three, it must remain a three, and must be placed back into its third position if required during the course of the game. If a player is unable to either add or subtract to equal any of the numbers left on their side of the tray they must replace a die by selecting any one of their dice removed earlier. If there are no dice to replace, you simply miss that turn (see example 19).

Roll Warning: Box Cars (double sixes), double fives and fours are unlucky rolls. You will have to either miss a turn or put a die back if these rolls occur.

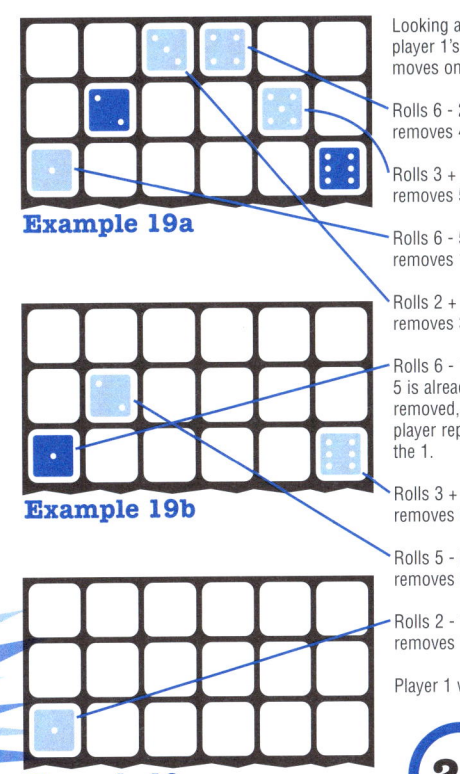

Example 19a

Example 19b

Example 19c

Looking at player 1's moves only:

Rolls 6 - 2, removes 4.

Rolls 3 + 2, removes 5.

Rolls 6 - 5, removes 1.

Rolls 2 + 1, removes 3.

Rolls 6 - 1, 5 is already removed, so player replaces the 1.

Rolls 3 + 3, removes 6.

Rolls 5 - 3, removes 2.

Rolls 2 - 1, removes 1.

Player 1 wins.

23

KNOCK YOURSELF OUT! (CONTINUED)

TO WIN

A Dicer must remove all six of their dice before their opponent.

POSSIBLE STRATEGY

Players need to learn the most probable combinations for adding and subtracting in order to increase the chances of winning the game. Remember, to be a "stratedizer" you need to make logical decisions based on previous outcomes. For example, when rolling two dice and allowing for both adding and subtracting combinations, how many ways can you roll the number <u>one</u>? Is it more probable to roll more combinations of <u>five</u>? You may need to keep track of all possible outcomes to form your conclusions.

SQUARE DOUBLING

2 DICERS OR 2 TEAMS 2 PLAY

This is a game for two Dicers or two teams of Dicers. Each Dicer needs their own gameboard so one player may choose the bottom of the tray and one may use the lid.

TO BEGIN

Players select 12 dice of their own colour. Dicers alternate rolling their dice one at a time and choose the best space to place their die.

THE GOAL

The goal of the game is to create the highest total sum of all twelve numbers in your square pattern. Check out example 20 to see the square pattern you will be building in your tray. You need to pay attention to this rule for sure! In order to have a row or column count, it must have a double number pattern (same number appears at least twice, ie., two 4's, two 6's, etc.). Once a player selects a space for their roll and it is placed into their tray, it cannot be moved, so be careful. Once both players have completed all their rolls, the scoring portion of the game begins.

Starting with the numbers in the corner squares, the sum for each "counting" row or column is calculated. Remember, only a row or column that includes at least one double number pattern can be calculated.

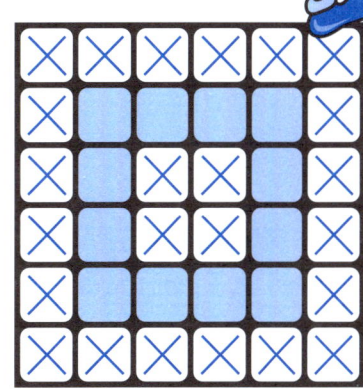

Example 20

The shaded area shows where a player can place their dice. The crossed out spaces are not used in this game.

25

SQUARE DOUBLING (CONTINUED)

Player 1 scores as follows:

Row 1: 14
(5+4+4+1=14)

Row 2: 12
(3+5+3+1=12)

Column 1: 0
(No Doubles)

Column 2: 10
(1+3+5+1=10)

Total Score: 36
(14+12+10=36)

Example 21

Check out Dicer one's board in example 21 to see what the total score would be. The Dicer with the highest total sum is the "KINGPIN" of Square Doubling. Awesome!!

VARIATION

To increase the difficulty, Dicers must have three of the same numbers per row or column and the gameboard will now change to a 6 x 6 grid, just like a frame. See below for further explanation.

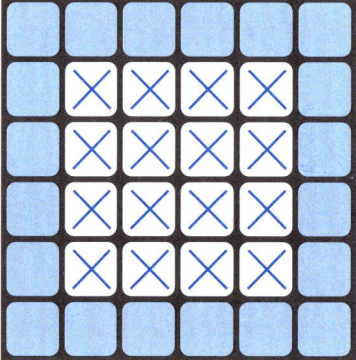

The shaded area shows where a player can place their dice. The crossed out spaces are not used in this variation.

3 OF A KIND is the name of the game for this variation

CHANCE

This is a game for two Dicers to play at one time. Players use one tray divided so that each player uses only their half.

TO BEGIN

Each Dicer chooses eighteen dice of their own colour and these are removed from the tray.

THE GOAL

The goal of the game is to correctly predict whether a die rolled will be greater than three or less than or equal to three.

Players alternate rolling their dice, making predictions and placing only the correctly guessed dice into their side of the tray.

EXAMPLE (see example 22)

Dicer one begins the play by predicting "Greater than" and then rolls a 2. Because 2 is less than 4, this die is placed aside and is not placed on player one's side of the tray to score later at the end of the game.

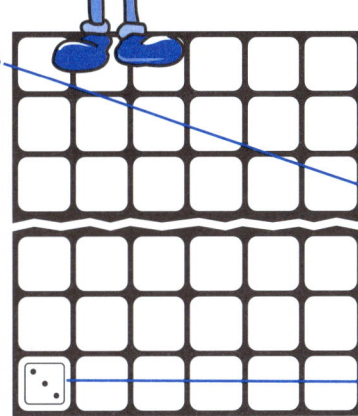

Example 22

Player 1 predicts "greater than" and rolls a 2. Player 1 is incorrect and the die is set aside.

Player 2 predicts "equal to" and rolls a 3. Player 2 is correct and places the die in the tray.

Play continues...

CHANCE (CONTINUED)

If players choose to total the value of all their dice, then player 1 has 26 and player 2 has 35. Player 2 wins.

If players choose to total the number of dice they were correct on, then player 1 has 9 dice and player 2 has 10 dice. Player 2 wins.

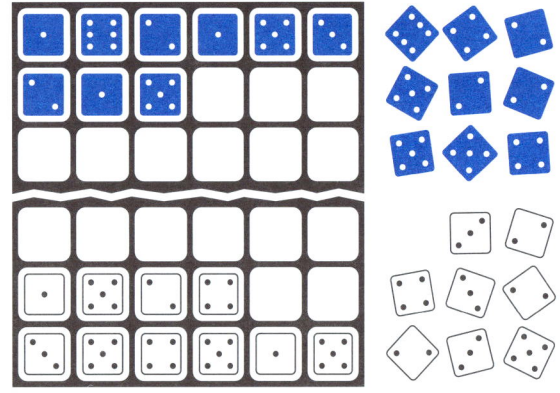

Example 23

Player two now predicts "Less than or equal to", rolls a 3 and because 3 is equal to the prediction, player two guessed correctly and places this die (with that number face up) into their side of the tray.

Dicers continue to alternate rolling all of their eighteen dice placing only those correctly guessed into their tray.

A RULE TWIST:

Goal of the game could be to predict whether the added sum of two dice rolled would be greater than 6 or equal to and less than 6, ie. 6 + 3 = 9 (if Dicer predicted "greater than", then these dice would be placed in their tray as the Dicer predicted correctly).

TO SCORE (see example 23)

Dicers could tally up the total value of all the dice in the tray or the Dicer with the most dice in their side of the tray wins. Remember, it's a game of chance so it's like flipping a coin, spinning a spinner, the luck of the draw... *yee ha!*

HIGH ROLLERS

This is a game for two Dicers to play at one time. Players use one tray divided so that each player uses only their half (see example 24).

2 DICERS 2 PLAY

TO BEGIN

Each Dicer chooses eighteen dice of their own colour and these are removed from the tray.

THE GOAL

The goal of the game is to build combinations that equal sums of either 5, 6 or 7. Player one begins by taking six of their dice and rolling all dice at once. Depending on what numbers were rolled, player one now decides whether to "build" combinations of dice that when added equal sums of 5, 6 or 7. Single dice rolled equalling 5 or 6 are also accepted and are considered good rolls.

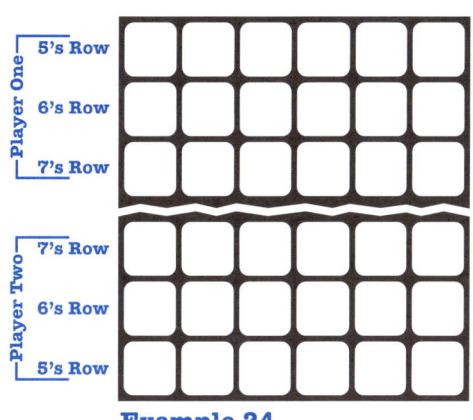

The tray is divided between the two players as shown.

Example 24

HIGH ROLLERS (CONTINUED)

EXAMPLE (see example 25)

Player 1 rolls:
3, 3, 4, 5, 3, 4
Player 1 chooses the 7's row and places both 3's and both 4's in the tray (3+4=7). Player 1 rolls twice more but cannot reach 7 again.

Player 2 rolls:
2, 3, 4, 1, 3, 4
Player 2 chooses the 5's row and places the 2, 3, 4 and 1 in the tray (2+3=5 and 4+1=5). Player 2 rolls again and rolls two 5's. Player 2 places both dice in the tray (each die equals 5).

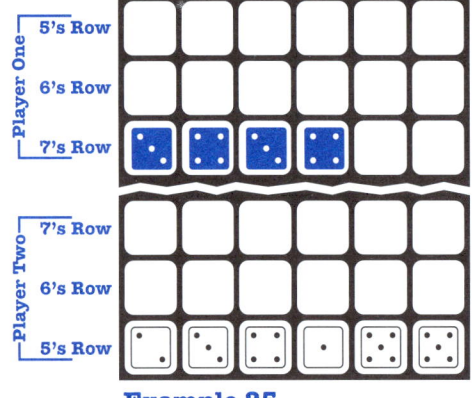

Example 25

If player one's first roll is as follows: 3, 3, 4, 5, 3, 4, then player one may choose to build SEVENS and would place the 3+4 and 3+4 aside. Player one now has two rolls left and chooses to re-roll the 5 and 3. Player one now rolls a 6 and 2 and chooses to re-roll these dice, taking their last roll. Player one rolls a 3 and 2 and these are placed aside and are now excluded from the remainder of the game.

Player two now takes their first turn by rolling six dice of their colour and after analyzing the roll, decides whether to build combinations of 5, 6 or 7.

ie. 2, 3, 4, 1, 3, 4

Player two now chooses to build their 5's and places the 2+3 and 4+1 dice into the first row (the 5's row on their side of the tray). Player two now re-rolls their 3 and 4 dice and now rolls two 5's. These dice are now also placed into the 5's row of their tray and the play now continues to player one who works on their five or six combinations. When both Dicers have filled their three rows, they now compare to see who has the highest total score (adding up the face value of all their own dice).

TO SPICE UP THE DICE

Try rolling combinations equalling 6, 7 and 8. Remember, strategy is the best policy!!!

DOUBLE TROUBLE

2 DICERS 2 PLAY

This is a game for two "Trouble Makers" or two teams of Dicers. Each Dicer or team needs their own tray. Don't forget - the lid can also become a playing board just like the bottom tray.

TO BEGIN

Each Dicer makes and records a guesstimate (which is really a calculated guess) as to how many pairs of double numbers they think they might roll. Dicers then take turns rolling all 36 dice and arrange their dice in pairs, by grouping them into their tray (see example 26).

Left over dice count as points against the Dicer. A score of ZERO would be best! The player must now compare their guesstimate to the actual amount of pairs that was rolled. If the Dicer guessed 18 pairs and only 17 pairs were rolled, then the difference of 1 would also be added to their score.

Dicer two or team two would now make their guesstimate, roll all 36 dice and arrange all possible pairs of doubles. Dicers continue to five rounds each and the player with the lowest score wins.

Remember, the lower the score, the less TROUBLE you'll get into!!

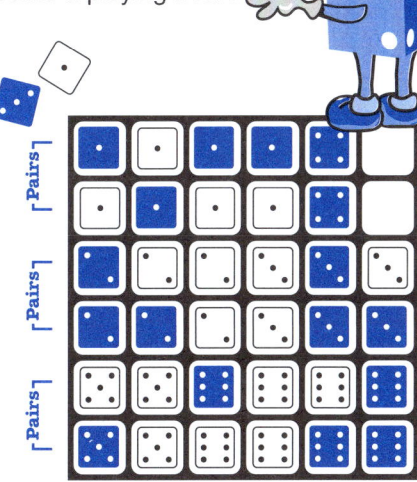

Player 1 guesses 18 pairs, then rolls all dice and arranges them into pairs in the tray. Player 1 ended up with 17 pairs and receives 1 point (18-17=1). There are also 2 dice left over, so player 1 receives 2 more points for a total of 3 points (2+1=3).

Example 26

31

4 BY 4

TWO PLAYERS SOLITAIRE

One Dicer uses the bottom tray and sixteen dice of their own colour and the other Dicer uses the lid of the tray and sixteen dice of their own colour.

TO BEGIN

The tray needs to be emptied of all 36 dice. Players will be building a 4 by 4 grid in their tray. Dicers roll their dice one by one, strategically placing their dice in any space of their gameboard.

Crossed out spaces are not used in this game.

Player 1 has two rolls remaining.

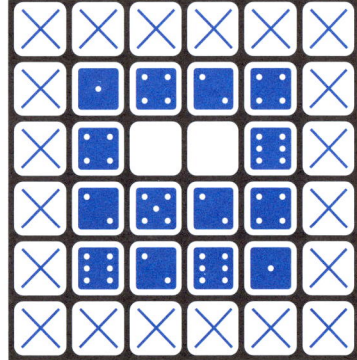

Example 27

THE GOAL

Dicers are placing their rolled dice into spaces where no two adjacent squares have consecutive numbers or the <u>same</u> number, ie. a 3 cannot be placed beside another 3, or a 2 or a 4. Likewise, a 1 cannot be placed beside another 1 or a 2. However, the numbers <u>can</u> be placed diagonally from one another. If a Dicer rolls a number that cannot successfully complete any intersecting row or column, they must choose the square which would be the most productive.

EXAMPLE (see example 27)

Dicer's tray is almost complete with two rolls left: Dicer now rolls a 5 and must choose the best "worst" square (meaning, one row or column will for sure not count, but perhaps one will).

4 BY 4 (CONTINUED)

If Dicer one chooses to place their 5 in the square on the right, ie. the vertical column of 2, 5, 2, 6 would still count for 1 point. However, if Dicer one chooses to place their 5 in the left square, ie. the vertical column of 4, 5, 5, 2 would <u>not</u> count for 1 point, nor would their horizontal row count (because 4 and 5 cannot be placed side by side).

TO SCORE (see example 28)

Each successful row and column is worth 1 point. The total score of 8 points is the highest possible score. If you can do this, you can do anything! You are the BEST DICER EVER!!

Remember... "Smart" Dicers are those that know how to make the best decision, whatever the throw of the die.

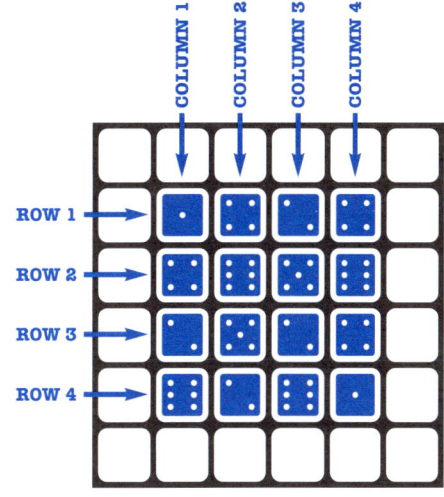

Player 1 receives 1 point for each successfully created row and/or column:

Columns 1, 3 and 4, and rows 1, 3 and 4 are all good, so Player 1 receives 6 points.

No points for column 2 because there is a 5 and 6 next to each other.

No points for row 2 because there is a 5 and 6 next to each other.

Example 28

HORSE RACE

This is a game for two Dicers to play at one time. Players use one tray divided so that each player uses only their half.

TO BEGIN

Each Dicer chooses eighteen dice of their own colour and these are removed from the tray.

THE GOAL

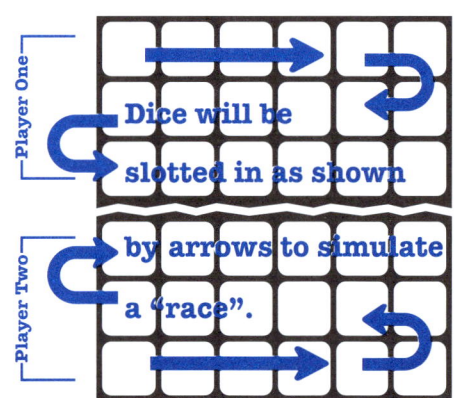

The tray is divided between the two players as shown.

The goal of the game is to have the most dice in your side of the "horse race track" after all dice have been rolled out for the round. Dicers roll two dice at one time.

Dicers add their two dice and compare their sums. The Dicer with the greatest sum places them into their side of the "horse race track". Their opponent places their two dice into the lid (losing side). Dicers pick up two new dice, roll, add and compare their sums. The Dicer with the greatest sum places them into their side of the "horse race track" and their opponent places them into the lid. In the event of a tie sum, both Dicers place their dice into their own side of the "horse race track". Dicers roll out all remaining dice. The Dicer with the most dice on their side of the "horse race track" after nine tosses, is the winner.

HORSE RACE (CONTINUED)

EXAMPLE

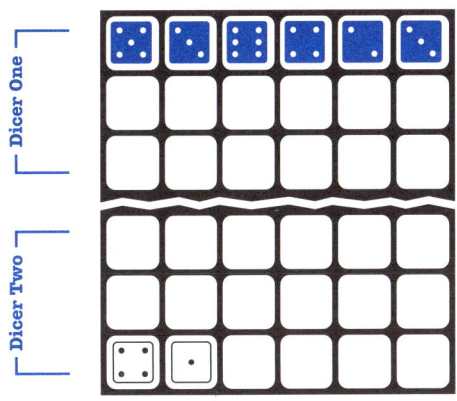

Play After 3 of 9 Rounds.

Toss 1

Dicer One :: + :: = 8 → WINS and places dice in tray

Dicer Two : + :. = 5 → Tosses dice into lid

Toss 2

Dicer One ::: + :: = 10 → WINS and places dice in tray

Dicer Two : + . = 3 → Tosses dice into lid

Toss 3

Dicer One : + :. = 5 → TIE both players place dice in tray

Dicer Two :: + . = 5

LEVEL 1

Play is outlined above, Dicers roll two dice and add.

HORSE RACE

LEVEL 2

Play as described in above rules, but now Dicers roll three dice and add for the greatest sum. The Dicer with the greatest sum (answer) places them into their side of the "horse race track".

+ + = 9

LEVEL 3

Play as described in above rules, but now Dicers roll two dice and multiply 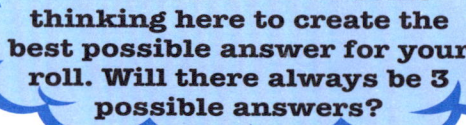 for the greatest product. The Dicer with the greatest product (answer) places them into their side of the "horse race track".

LEVEL 4

Play as described in above rules, but now Dicers roll three dice, add two, and multiply by the third for the greatest product. **See example.**

The Dicer with the greatest product places them into their side of the "horse race track".

(5 + 3) x 6 = 48 ☆ Best Choice
(6 + 3) x 5 = 45
(6 + 5) x 3 = 33

You will have to do some thinking here to create the best possible answer for your roll. Will there always be 3 possible answers?